*Twenty bridges from Tower to Kew –*
*Wanted to know what the River knew,*
*Twenty Bridges or twenty-two,*
*For they were young, and the Thames was old*
*And this is the tale that River told: ...*

'I remember the bat-winged lizard-birds,
The Age of Ice and the Mammoth herds,
And the giant tigers that stalked them down
Through Regent's Park into Camden Town.
And I remember like yesterday
The earliest Cockney who came my way,
When he pushed through the forest that lined the Strand,
With paint on his face and a club in his hand.
He was death to feather and fin and fur.
He trapped my beavers at Westminster.
He netted my salmon, he hunted my deer,
He killed my heron off Lambeth Pier ...

Rudyard Kipling, *The River's Tale* (Prehistoric)

# PREHISTORIC COOKERY

## Recipes & History

by
### Jane Renfrew

with a Foreword by
### Loyd Grossman OBE

ENGLISH HERITAGE

*Front cover:* A charging bison depicted in a cave at Altamira in Spain, c 13,000 BC

To Barbara,
        with lots of love from Wyn,
to fill in any gaps in your
extensive library of cookery books!
September, 2008

Published by English Heritage, 23 Savile Row, London W1S 2ET

Copyright © English Heritage and Jane Renfrew
First published 1985
Revised edition 2005

ISBN 1 85074 934 5

Product code 51030

Edited by Susan Kelleher, Publishing, English Heritage, Kemble Drive, Swindon SN2 2GZ
Designed by Pauline Hull
Printed in England by The Bath Press, Bath

# CONTENTS

# FOREWORD

Would the pyramids have been built without the recently invented bread to efficiently feed the workforce? Food is a common denominator between us all, and a potent link with our ancestors, just as much as an ancient parish church or a listed house.

I am delighted to contribute a Foreword to English Heritage's series of historic cookery books, which neatly combine two of my passions – history and food. Most of us no longer have to catch or grow our own food before eating it, but the continuing daily need for sustenance still powerfully links us with our earliest forebears. We may not like the thought of Roman fish sauce made from fermented entrails (until we next add oyster sauce to a Chinese beef dish), but we can only sigh with recognition at a Jacobean wife's exhortation to 'let yor butter bee scalding hott in yor pan' before pouring in the beaten eggs for an omelette. The Roman penchant for dormice cooked in milk doesn't resonate with us now, but a dish of pears in red wine features at modern dinner parties just as it did in medieval times.

Food and cooking have inevitably changed down the centuries, as modern cookers have supplanted open hearths, and increased wealth and speedy transport have opened up modern tastes and palates to the widest range of ingredients and cuisines. But it's worth remembering that it was the Romans who gave us onions, sugar was an expensive luxury in the 16th century as was tea in the 17th, the tomato only became popular in Europe in the 19th century and even in the 1950s avocados and red peppers were still exotic foreign imports.

I urge you to experiment with the recipes in these books which cover thousands of years, and hope you enjoy, as I have, all that is sometimes strange and often familiar about the taste of times past.

**Loyd Grossman** OBE
Former Commissioner of English Heritage
Chairman of the Campaign for Museums

# INTRODUCTION

Many people might imagine that the task of reconstructing the diet of our prehistoric ancestors would be completely impossible. In some ways they are right, but when archaeologists recover the remains of our distant forebears and their tools, they also look for clues about their foods. The process is essentially one of detective work and the direct evidence may survive in a variety of different forms: as mounds of discarded sea shells, the bones of wild and domestic animals (sometimes showing butchery marks, traces of burning during cooking, or split to obtain the marrow). The remains of plants are also often preserved mainly as seeds or fruits, having been charred in the past or buried in other conditions which favour preservation, as in waterlogged soils, or else having been preserved as impressions in clay vessels or in daub. So whether it be the hunters of the Palaeolithic period, the first farmers of Neolithic times or the Celtic chieftains of the late Iron Age, we have quite a number of clues to help us reconstruct their diet. But having

*Opposite:* A reconstructed Iron Age house at Butser Ancient Farm, near Petersfield, Hampshire

discovered the ingredients which were available, our task is to work out what could have been made from them.

A further lead in this quest is given by studying the tools used for food preparation – for cutting, grinding, pounding and for cooking. Thus we can begin to understand the range of cooking techniques which were available at any given time in our prehistoric past, and to see how they developed through time.

Another aid in reconstructing the methods used by prehistoric cooks is to examine the different practices which have survived in the more remote parts of the British Isles, where the inhabitants had to make do with much the same ingredients as were available in later prehistory. The ingenuity of the islanders of Orkney and Shetland, for example, serves to remind us that when the ingredients were limited in range it was up to the cook to make them varied, interesting and palatable. The recipes which follow have drawn on their experience.

The first men appear to have arrived in Britain sometime before 300,000 years ago. These men were hunters and lived in the Pleistocene period when Britain was subjected to the advances of the polar icecap which reached as far south as London. When it periodically retreated, however, the interglacial periods were extremely warm. Naturally, these huge changes in climate and vegetation led to a great variation in the sorts of animals and plants which formed the food supply of the hunters and gatherers. In the cold phases the exposed parts of southern Britain appear to have been roamed by mammoth, woolly rhinoceros, reindeer, bison, musk ox and arctic hare. In the warmer interglacials these species were replaced by the straight-tusked elephant, the Clacton fallow deer, bear, wild oxen, red deer, rhinoceros, hyena and even, in

Prehistoric painting of a male and female deer

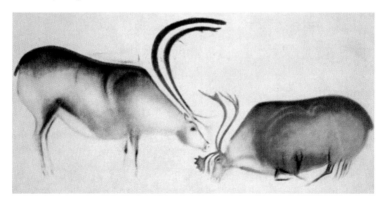

some places, hippopotamus. Their bones have been found in association with the characteristic flint hand-axe tools of these early Stone Age hunters. There has been little evidence for the plant food part of their diet, but we can assume that it was probably similar to modern hunting communities and would be up to 80 per cent of their diet.

A 19th-century painting by Emmanuel Benner of a prehistoric family hunting a bear

These hunters led a nomadic life following the herds of animals which they relied on for meat, and this pattern of shifting hunters and gatherers continued to occupy Britain throughout the Palaeolithic. Their tool kit gradually improved by making their hunting weapons more effective with projectile points, and

A flint arrowhead discovered at Irthlingborough, Northamptonshire

they began to make sharp flint knives from long blades struck from the cores. At the end of the Palaeolithic, many of the inhabitants in Britain were living in caves and were hunting horses, reindeer, giant Irish deer, elk, arctic fox, woolly rhino and mammoth.

With the retreat of the ice sheets the climate became progressively milder, and after about 10,000 BC the tundra vegetation gave way to a forested environment – first of birch, hazel and pine and then of oak and other deciduous trees such as elm, lime and alder. With the spread of the forests, the large herds of wild animals were replaced by forest species such as the red and roe deer, elk, wild oxen and wild boar. Hunters who lived close to the sea also began to exploit shellfish and sea fish, leaving huge mounds of shells and fish-bones as evidence of their taste for marine foods. Thus from about 300,000 to about 3500 BC the inhabitants of Britain lived exclusively by hunting and gathering.

About 3500 BC the first farmers reached Britain from the continent by sea (the land bridge which had joined us to Europe during the Palaeolithic period had become submerged after the melting of the ice sheets before 6000 BC). These early farmers brought bags of seed corn with them comprising two types of hulled wheat (emmer and einkorn), and the hulled and naked forms of six-row barley, and flax. They also brought young domestic cattle, sheep, goats and pigs. Their completely new lifestyle included living in more or less permanent settlements using pottery containers, weaving cloth, making polished stone tools and constructing elaborate tombs and ritual monuments. Their arrival brought a truly fundamental change in the way of life of the inhabitants of Britain, and they laid the foundations of society as we know it today. These first farmers set the stage for various technological developments, the most important of which was the development of metallurgy – first with the making of copper, then bronze tools and

*Opposite:* A reconstruction painting by Judith Dobie showing what Chysauster Ancient Village might have looked like in the Iron Age

later with iron working too. These had implications for cooking since it was now possible to have a wider range of tools, especially sharper knives, and later buckets and cauldrons, flesh-hooks, firedogs, spits and tripods, spoons and elegant drinking vessels.

The recipes which follow are supposed to reflect the development of the prehistoric economy in Britain, but several practical restraints have had to be introduced. First, it is rather difficult to give recipes which might relate to the Palaeolithic period since it is clearly difficult to obtain the ingredients – mammoth steaks or rhinoceros joints for example! So I have confined the recipes to the early post-glacial period and from then on to the end of the Iron Age immediately preceding the Roman invasion. I have also included only those wild foods which can be fairly easily recognised and are relatively abundant, so that anyone following the recipes will not subject themselves to the misfortune of consuming unpalatable or even poisonous plants by mistake, or to collecting plants which, though once common, are now rare and should be conserved.

The main difference between prehistoric food and that of today is that our distant ancestors cooked rather simply; they did not go in for elaborate sauces and, having few ovens, did not bake pies. Also, a number of important ingredients which we use today were not available to them including yeast (except the wild forms), baking powder, cream of tartar, spices, lemons, oranges, grapes, wine, vinegar, olive oil, onions, tomatoes, potatoes and cornflour. They did not have sugar but used honey for sweetening.

They did, however, use wild vegetation far more than we do now and their edible plants probably reflected seasonal availability to a greater extent. One reason for this is that deep freezing and freeze-drying preserve our vegetables out of season; in the past vegetables and fruits could only be preserved by air-drying, or by making them into jam or jelly, or alcoholic beverages such as mead. As far as we know most vegetable foodstuffs were not preserved on a large scale outside their season of availability. The only exception to this was grain, which was stored in pits to provide a steady food supply through the winter and up to the next harvest.

The same problem of preservation also affected animal products. Meat and fish could be air-dried, sun-dried, salted or smoked to preserve them through the scarce winter months, and this has been practised until recent times in the islands off our northern coasts.

Another feature that strikes us when looking at the uses of animals, birds and fish in these remote places is that nothing was wasted; udder, lights, tripe, brains, head, feet, tails, blood and even gristle were made into dishes which may not sound appetising to our rather refined notions today, but which would be quite acceptable in the absence of any alternatives.

*Opposite:* Remains of Chysauster Ancient Village, Cornwall

| TIMELINE | |
|---|---|
| **Pliocene** | period of geological time about **5.2 – 1.6 million years ago** |
| **Pleistocene** | period of geological time from the end of the Pliocene up to about 10,000 years ago. Also known as the **Great Ice Age** |
| **Palaeolithic** | term for human cultures during the Pleistocene (Lower, Middle and Upper) **800,000 – 10,000** BC |
| **Mesolithic** | 10,000 – 4400 BC |
| **Neolithic** | 4400 – 2500 BC |
| **Bronze Age** | 2500 – 800 BC |
| **Iron Age** | 800 BC to the Roman invasion in AD 43 |

# ROCK ART

A group of small horses painted in the caves at Lascaux, France

Horses, rhinos, bison and deer are just a few of the many animals painted by prehistoric artists on the walls of caves throughout Europe. It is astonishing that, despite being many thousands of years old, these paintings are still full of freshness and vigour and it is obvious that the people who created them were skilled painters. Not only are the animals portayed accurately but many of them also seem three-dimensional due to a clever use of the texture of the rock face.

It was not until the 1860s that the first paintings were discovered and it took several decades before they were accepted as genuine by anthropologists and art historians. Unfortunately, when some of the caves were opened the paintings rapidly deteriorated in the air, but those that survive provide a fascinating glimpse of prehistoric society.

Hunting scenes are often depicted in the paintings and some of the animals are vast – in the world-famous caves at Lascaux in France there is a 6 metre (20 ft) bull. The artists had to work in extremely difficult conditions – at Altamira in Spain the caves are so low that they would have needed to squat all the time, while at Labastide in the Pyrenees they are so tall that scaffolding would have been needed to paint the immense horse some 4.5 metres (15 ft) above the floor.

The first paintings were done in red and black only but later a wide spectrum of colours was used by combining different minerals. The individual colours were often placed in small containers – barnacle shells being ideal for the purpose. All sorts of methods were used to apply the paint to the cave wall – brushes made of animal hair or leaves, stencils and even spraying through bird bones.

The paintings must have been a real labour of love and a source of much wonder to our ancestors – as indeed they are today.

Bison painted around 15,000 BC in the caves at Altamira in Spain

*Recipes*

# FISH SOUP

**Trimmings and head of a
    large fish**
**1 small haddock**
**salt**
**seasoning (optional)**
**flour**
**milk**

Thoroughly clean the trimmings and
put in a pan with the haddock. Cover
with cold, salted water. Bring slowly to
the boil and skim. Add seasoning
(if using), simmer for 40 minutes, strain
and return liquid to the pan. For every
1.1 litres (2 pints) of stock mix 30 ml
(2 tbls) flour to a paste with some
milk and add to the soup to thicken it.
Bring to the boil, check seasoning
and serve.

# HAKKA MUGGIES

**1 fish stomach (a ling muggie
    is best)**
**1 cod liver**
**seasoning**
**oatmeal**

Wash the muggie carefully and tie the
small end tightly with string. Break up
or slice the cod liver, season well, and
fill the muggie with alternate layers of
liver and oatmeal until two-thirds full.
Close, leaving enough room for the
oatmeal to swell, and tie tightly with
string. Plunge into boiling salted water
and boil gently for 25–30 minutes.
Remove from the water, and serve hot
with bread.

## GRILLED HADDOCK

Have ready a clear red fire; allow one
medium haddock per person. Gut the
fish and then lay them across the hot
embers. Grill first on one side, then
turn over and grill the other side.
Rub with a pat of butter and serve
immediately. The haddock may also be
toasted in front of the fire, retaining all
the juices and flavour of the fish.

## SLOTT

**1 cod roe**
**flour**
**salt**

Beat the roe until creamy, then add a little flour and salt and form them into small dumplings. Drop them into boiling, well-salted water, and cook for 20–25 minutes. When ready they will rise to the top. Eat hot or, when cold, cut into slices and fry in butter.

## BOILED SAMPHIRE

Samphire is a great delicacy. Pick the marsh samphire during July or August at low tide. It should be carefully washed soon after collection and is best eaten very fresh. Tie the washed samphire, with the roots still intact, in bundles and boil in shallow, unsalted water for 8–10 minutes. Cut the string and serve with melted butter. Eat the samphire by picking each stem up by the root and biting lightly, pulling the fleshy part away from the woody core.

# CARRAGHEEN SWEET MOUSSE

**7 g ('/4 oz) dried carragheen**
**575 ml (1 pt) milk**
**1 egg, separated**
**15 g ('/2 oz) sugar or honey**

To serve:
**Decorate with fresh raspberries (optional)**

Soak the dried carragheen for 15 minutes in water, then pick out the dried ends and discard the water. Add the carragheen to the milk in a saucepan and slowly bring to the boil. Simmer for about 10 minutes, or until the mixture is quite thick. Beat the egg yolk with the honey or sugar. Strain the carragheen mixture and add the honey mixture to it. Beat the egg white until stiff, then fold into the mixture, stirring well, and pour into a bowl to set. The mousse takes 2–3 hours to set. It is nice to eat by itself, but is excellent with fresh or stewed fruit. If you omit the egg, the mixture will set just as well and make a nourishing blancmange.

# LAVERBREAD

*Laver is an edible seaweed that is found on the west coast of Britain.*

Collect a good basketful of laver, avoiding any that are sandy. Break up the large pieces and wash thoroughly in cold water. Cook steadily for about 4 hours in a large pan of boiling water, checking every 30 minutes that it does not boil dry. It is cooked when the sheets of laver have broken into tiny pieces, forming a smooth purée that is known as laverbread. Drain away excess liquid and store the puréed laverbread in the fridge until required. It will keep fresh for about a week. It is best served warm on fried bread garnished with bacon, since this helps to complement the unusual texture and appearance of this excellent food.

Edible seaweeds. Left: green laver; centre: dulse; right: devil's apron

# FRIED PIKE

1 pike, weighing 1.4–1.8 kg
  (3–4 lb)
salt
flour
1 egg, beaten
dry breadcrumbs

Scale and clean the pike thoroughly removing the head and tail. Cut the fish into slices and cover with very cold water. Remove when the fish feels firm. Dry well and rub lightly with salt and flour. Brush the slices of pike with the beaten egg, then coat in breadcrumbs. Fry in shallow fat for about 30 minutes until tender.

# GRILLED SALMON

2–3 slices of middle cut salmon
30 ml (2 tbls) melted butter
salt

To garnish:
parsley butter

Wipe the fish with a damp cloth, then brush with melted butter. Season with salt to taste. Place the fish slices on a well-greased grill rack and grill for 6–8 minutes on each side according to thickness. Serve immediately, garnished with parsley butter.

# ROAST VENISON

Venison is inclined to be hard and dry unless carefully cooked. Lard the joint and tie a jacket of fat pork round it to retain the moisture. It may be roasted on a spit, but it is probably more convenient to roast it in the oven at gas mark 4, 180°C (350°F), allowing 30 minutes per 450 g (1 lb). Serve with wild mushrooms and rowan jelly.

Late Bronze Age cauldron

# MARROW BONES

**225 g (8 oz) marrow bones
  per serving**
**flour**
**salt**

To serve:
**dry toast**

Scrape and wash the bones and saw in half across the shaft (the butcher will do this for you). Make a stiff paste of flour and water and roll it out. Cover the ends of the bones with the paste to seal in the marrow, and then tie the bones in a floured cloth. Stand upright in a pan of boiling salted water and simmer slowly for about 2 hours, refilling the pan with boiling water if necessary. Untie the cloth and remove the paste from each bone. Fasten a paper napkin round each one and serve with dry toast

## ROAST GOOSE

**50 g (2 oz) butter**
**salt**
**1 young goose**
   **(up to 4 months old)**

To garnish:
**watercress**

Mix the butter and salt together and place inside the bird. Truss and cook in a moderate oven, gas mark 4, 180–190°C (350–375°F) for about 1 hour, basting if necessary. Instead of roasting in an oven, the goose could be roasted over an open fire. Place the cooked bird on a serving dish and garnish with watercress.

## GRILLED OX TAILS

**2 ox tails**
**850 ml (1 1/2 pt) well-flavoured**
   **stock**
**1 egg, beaten**
**dry breadcrumbs, for coating**
**melted butter**

Wash and dry the ox tails and divide them into pieces at the joints. Put into a saucepan with the stock. Simmer gently for 2 1/2 hours or until tender. Drain well and leave until cold. Dip the ox tail pieces into the egg, then coat with the breadcrumbs. Brush with melted butter and grill until browned all over.

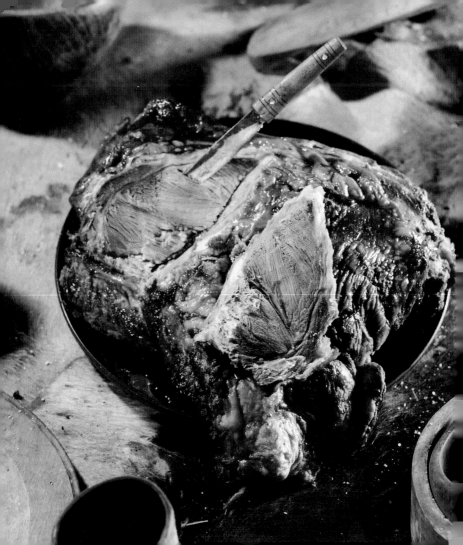

# GRILLED BREAST OF MUTTON

**1 breast of mutton**
**salt**

Divide the breast into serving portions. Remove surplus fat and skin and season the mutton with salt. Grill quickly under a hot grill or over hot embers to seal the surface, then reduce the heat and grill for a further 15–20 minutes, turning the meat frequently.

# CUTLETS OF WILD BOAR

Sauté the cutlets in oil or butter until tender, and arrange them on croutons of fried bread. Pour over them the pan juices mixed with a little cream and a few crushed juniper berries (1–2 per cutlet). Serve with unsweetened apple sauce.

# NETTLE PURÉE

Put young nettle tops into boiling water and boil until tender. Drain well and chop finely. Reheat, adding butter and salt to taste. Sorrel, dandelion, spinach, sow thistle, watercress and lady's smock may all be mixed for this purée (if the more bitter herbs – dandelion and sow thistle – are used alone, change the water after 5 minutes boiling). Cooking in a liberal amount of fast-boiling water will conserve the vitamins better than slow, gentle cooking.

# PEASE PUDDING

*Originally the peas were probably tied in a floured cloth and hung to cook in the cauldron in which a large piece of pork was being boiled.*

**250 g (8 oz) dried green peas, soaked overnight**
**a few sprigs of mint and thyme**
**25 g (1 oz) butter**
**salt**

Boil the peas in water with the herbs until soft and the skins are well loosened. Drain thoroughly and put through a sieve or blender with the butter. Add salt to taste. Press into a well-greased pudding basin, cover tightly with foil and steam for 1 hour. Turn out carefully, and serve with meat.

## SOWANS OR VIRPA

**450 g (I lb) fine oatmeal**
**1.4 kg (3 lb) wheatmeal**
**9 l (16 pt) water**

Put both meals in a stone crock. Stir in 8 litres (14 pints) lukewarm water and let it stand for 5–8 days until sour. Pour off the clear liquid and let this stand a few more days until rather sharp: this is the swats, which makes a refreshing drink. The remainder in the crock will resemble thick starch. Add about 1 litre (2 pints) water to give the consistency of cream. Strain through a cheesecloth over a colander. The liquid which is passed through will contain all the nutritious properties of oatmeal, with only the husk remaining. Gentle rubbing with a wooden spoon and a final squeezing of the cloth by hand will hasten the process. This dish is good for invalids.

## EASTER LEDGE PUDDING

**450 g (I lb) young bistort leaves**
**and nettle tops (dandelion**
**leaves and lady's mantle may**
**also be used for added flavour)**
**125 g (4 oz) pot barley, washed**
**salt**
**I egg**
**a large knob of butter**

Chop the greens and sprinkle the washed barley among them, adding some salt. Boil in a muslin bag for about 2 hours. Before serving, beat the mixture in a bowl with the egg, butter and salt to taste. Form into cakes and fry in shallow fat. Recommended as a good spring tonic.

## FRUMENTY

Half fill a jar with wheat grains, wash them, then cover with milk or water and set in a warm oven for 12 hours. The grains will swell and burst, and in this state are known as creed wheat. Frumenty may be eaten with cream and honey.

## BURSTIN AND MILK

Burstin is made from hulled six-row barley grains which are dried in a pot by the fire until roasted and then hand ground on a quern, making a rich brown meal. Put the burstin meal in a basin, heat some milk and pour over. Serve hot. This may also be made with cold milk or with buttermilk.

A reconstruction painting by Ivan Lapper of the Late Bronze Age settlement at Grimspound, Devon

# PORRIDGE

**575 ml (1 pt) water**
**a pinch of salt**
**50 g (2 oz) oatmeal**

To serve:
**milk and honey (optional)**

Bring the water to the boil and add
the salt. Sprinkle in the oatmeal very
gradually, stirring well after each addition,
then bring to the boil. Boil gently for
20 minutes if using fine oatmeal or
30 minutes for coarse. Serve with
cold milk and honey if desired.

# TANSY PUDDING

**275 ml (1/2 pt) milk**
**15 g (1/2 oz) butter**
**75 g (3 oz) fresh white**
    **breadcrumbs**
**25 g (1 oz) sugar or honey**
**10 ml (2 tsps) finely chopped**
    **tansy leaves**
**2 eggs, beaten**

To serve:
**honey and cream**

Boil the milk and butter together and
pour over the breadcrumbs. Set aside
for 30 minutes. Add the sugar or
honey and the tansy leaves to the
eggs, then mix with the breadcrumbs
and bake the mixture in a moderate
oven, gas mark 4, 180°C (350°F) until
set. Eat cold with honey and cream.

## YORKSHIRE RIDDLE BREAD

Mix a quantity of pinhead oatmeal with water to make a thick porridge. Leave overnight in a warm room. Next day add salt to taste and place spoonfuls on to a hot bakestone or griddle. As the bread cools it bubbles up giving a characteristic appearance. Brown the cakes on one side only.

## BLAANDA BREAD

**150 ml (10 tbls) barley meal**
**150 ml (10 tbls) oatmeal**
**a pinch of salt**
**50 g (2 oz) butter**
**milk, to mix**

Mix the two meals and the salt in a bowl, then rub in the fat. Gradually add the milk to make a dough which is firm but not sticky. Shape into a round flat bannock and bake slowly on a griddle over the fire.

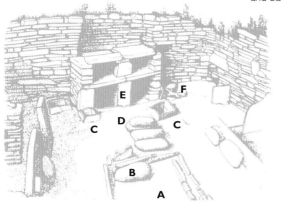

Interior of a Neolithic house at Skara Brae in Orkney.

**A** Hearth
**B** Bakestone
**C** Water-tight stone boxes
**D** Saddle quern
**E** Stone dresser
**F** Knocking stone

# FLOWERPOT BREAD

**600 g (1 lb 6 oz) wheatmeal flour**
**15 g ('/2 oz) leaven (see below)**
**15 g ('/2 oz) salt**
**about 350–425 ml (12–15 fl oz)**
**   milk and water, mixed**

For these quantities use two terracotta flowerpots, about 14 cm (5'/2 ins) in diameter. Temper the pots by coating with oil and putting into a hot oven. Repeat the process three or four times. Once the pots are well sealed they will need very little greasing.

Mix the ingredients together to make a dough. Leave to rise for 2 hours, work the dough, then leave to rise again for a further 2 hours. Divide the risen dough between the pots and leave to prove

for 45 minutes. Invert on a baking sheet and bake for 30 minutes at gas mark 7–8, 220–230°C (425–450°F). Remove the pots, reduce the heat to gas mark 2'/2–4, 160–180°C (320–350°F) and bake for 10–15 minutes more.

*Leaven*: Mix a small quantity of barley flour with warm water to make a dough. Form into a round shape and make a dent in the centre to go about halfway through. Put the dough on a plate, cross it lightly with a knife twice and fill the dent with warm water. Set it aside for a few days when the dough will have fermented and split like an overripe fruit. It is then ready to use as yeast to 'plum' the bread.

*Opposite*: A reconstruction painting by Judith Dobie of an Iron Age homestead

# History

# PREHISTORIC FOOD RESOURCES

The sea and seashore were important sources of food for those who lived near. The occasional stranding of whales round the coasts must have provided a great bonus to those living in the vicinity, and it is not uncommon for up to four whales on average to be stranded on British shores each year. Olaus Magnus, writing in 1555, described how a single whale might fill between 250 and 300 waggons and yield meat for salting, blubber for lighting and heating, small bones for fuel and large ones for housebuilding, and hide sufficient to clothe 40 men – so it is easy to understand what a windfall such a stranding might be. Perhaps the earliest example of human exploitation of this resource is from Meiklewood near Stirling in Scotland where a Mesolithic deer antler mattock was found propped against the skull of a Rorqual whale. Seals were also exploited off the Scottish coast and their bones occur in the Mesolithic middens in Argyll and on Oronsay.

The Mesolithic inhabitants of Oronsay already practised deep-sea fishing from boats; they caught and ate conger eel, sea bream, saithe, wrasse, haddock, thornback ray, skate and shark.

At Morton, Fife, on the east coast of Scotland, the Mesolithic fishermen were also catching cod, salmon and sturgeon. In the Orkney Islands during the Neolithic period, they were catching cod and coalfish; and finds of crushed fish-bones in a mortar at Skara Brae may suggest that fishmeal was used as a famine food. Fish was probably best eaten fresh, being gutted and grilled over an open fire, or baked in hot embers. A large fish would be cut into steaks to facilitate quick and even cooking. Fish roes and livers also constituted rich foods much valued in the Northern Isles.

Crabs and lobsters were collected along the edge of the shoreline, or just beyond it, probably in weighted baskets – the forerunners of modern lobster pots. They were certainly appreciated by the Mesolithic inhabitants of Oronsay and Oban, and have probably been valued ever since.

Around the shores of Britain are a series of sites which consist of huge middens of shells, the discarded remains of many meals of shellfish which have been widely valued by the communities living by or visiting the seashore. This is not quite universally true since in Orkney they have traditionally regarded 'ebb meat' as a last resource in times of hardship. Gathering shellfish may well be

regarded as rather labour intensive. The most common species represented are oysters, limpets, mussels, and winkles. It has been argued that the limpets may have been used as fishing bait, but since they are found in such large numbers some at least may have been used for food, possibly as a tasty addition to a fish stew or soup. Sea urchins were also used for food on the late Neolithic/early Bronze Age site at Northton, Harris. All these shellfish are best cooked by dropping them into boiling water and boiling them briskly before extracting them from their shells. They may also be roasted on hot stones. As soon as the shells open a piece of butter is put inside each, and the shellfish eaten immediately.

Sea birds also formed an important source of food on the coastal sites. Guillemots were present in the Mesolithic site at Morton, Fife. They were also present at Skara Brae in Orkney,

Oysters and mussels – a valued part of the prehistoric diet

and on the Rousay sites where gannets, eider ducks and their eggs, pink-footed geese, and swans were also in evidence. There is no doubt that these birds were valued for food as well as for their feathers. The inhabitants of St Kilda in the 18th century caught guillemots and gannets and either ate them fresh or salted them for use during the long winter months. They also ate large quantities of the birds' eggs boiled.

No finds of seaweed are known from early sites but it is likely that laver (*Porphyra umbilicalis*), which grows in the intertidal zone on the rocky coasts of western Britain, and also carragheen or Irish moss (*Chondrus crispus*), were probably both used, as they are today. Both species are rich in iodine and vitamins. Seakale (*Crambe maritima*), a plant growing on the shingle beaches round the British shores yields delicate, tender shoots which can be cooked and eaten like asparagus, and marsh samphire (*Salicornia europaea*), which grows on the sandy mud of salt marshes, has succulent fleshy stems of delicate flavour when boiled. Both these plants may have been locally exploited but would leave no archaeological trace.

Inland, the hunters of the early post-glacial forests relied heavily on game animals for their meat supply. The Mesolithic band which camped during the spring beside a lake at Star Carr, Yorkshire, were hunting red and roe deer, elk, wild ox and wild pig with the occasional wolf, pine marten, hedgehog and badger. The presence of domestic dog at this site suggests that it was used by the hunters in their food quest.

With the coming of agriculture, hunting still played a significant role in the seasonal food supply. Elk disappeared by Neolithic times, and wild oxen by the end of that period. The Neolithic farmers hunted wild ox, especially in southern Britain where their bones are often found associated with Neolithic monuments. The commonest animal hunted, however, was the red deer, found on sites from the Orkneys to Dorset. Not only was it an important source of food, but it also supplied the huge numbers of antlers used as tools in the flint mines and in the construction of earthworks. In general the red deer appear to have been much larger than contemporary Scottish deer. Of the other species of deer, both roe and fallow deer have been

A stag's antler discovered at Silbury Hill, Wiltshire. This was probably used in the construction of this prehistoric mound

found on Neolithic sites in the south and east of the country. Wild horse, wild boar, brown bear and beaver have also been found on Neolithic sites.

At Glastonbury, Somerset, during the Iron Age the farmers hunted red and roe deer, wild boar, fox, wild cat, otter and beaver,

as well as hedgehog, marten, weasel and polecat. It was probably in the Iron Age that hunting was first regarded as a sport with the Celtic warriors decorating their shields with wild boar emblems to show their prowess in the hunt.

The meat of these game animals would have been eaten at once – or else hung for a long while to tenderise and then eaten 'high' as it still is today. It seems that all parts of game animals were eaten in some form or other. The gut may well have been used as a container for liver, lights and brains cut up and mixed with fat, and then either slowly roasted over the embers of a fire, or boiled; it is a type of dish which survives as the Scottish haggis.

It is possible that the early hunters ate the half-digested contents of the stomachs of their quarry. They certainly broke open the mandibles and long bones of the animals they hunted to extract the marrow.

Of the wild birds hunted in the late Upper Palaeolithic period, the bones found at Kent's Cavern, Torquay, Devon, show that grouse, ptarmigan, grey-lag goose and whooper swan were being hunted for food. The first farmers also hunted geese, swans and ducks. It is possible that the art of falconry began to be practised during the Bronze Age as an aid in catching birds for food. There are a number of burials in Yorkshire where an archer is buried together with a hawk's head, for example, in the beaker grave at Kelleythorpe.

The long list of birds, predominantly aquatic species, which were hunted by the Iron Age fowlers of the Somerset Lake Villages include: pelican, cormorant, heron, bittern, puffin, whooper swan, goose, wild duck, golden eye, teal, widgeon, pintail, shoveler, tufted duck, scaup, common pochard, red-breasted merganser and common crane. At Meare the bones of black and red grouse and partridge were also found. Birds' eggs were also important in the diet, in the long centuries before the introduction of the domestic fowl sometime in the later Iron Age.

The Mesolithic fishermen on the inland waterways caught freshwater fish such as pike by using fish spears or leisters armed with barbed antler points. Fish hooks were not introduced till much later. Fish traps and the use of fish nets have a long prehistory. At Glastonbury, lead net sinkers were quite common and the villagers caught roach, perch, shad and trout. Pike and salmon were still caught using fish spears since they are much larger fish.

*Opposite:* A pair of grouse – still as much of a delicacy today as they were thousands of years ago

The first domestic animals arrived in Britain around 3500 BC with the first farmers. They must have brought young animals in their skin boats across the Channel. Herds of sheep, goats, cattle and pigs were soon established. There may have been some subsequent crossing between the long-horned domestic cattle and the wild ox of the native forest before that species died out at the end of the Neolithic period. A small breed of goat was identified in the animal bones from Windmill Hill, Wiltshire, and the sheep appear to have resembled the long-tailed Drenthe breed of Dutch heath sheep. The pig is also of a small form which persisted in Britain until the Iron Age. Both cattle and pigs would be happy browsing in the clearings in the forest but the sheep and goats would thrive better on the well-drained uplands. There is no evidence for the domestication of the horse before the Bronze Age. The Neolithic dogs were of the large fox-terrier type.

Cattle appear to have been the most significant of the Neolithic domestic animals. At many of the causewayed camps in southern Britain large numbers of young animals (under the age of one year) appear to have been pole-axed – presumably to provide veal for eating. Many of their bones show knife cuts at points suitable for the removal of sinew, flesh and skin, and many of the bones were also split for the extraction of marrow. The high proportion of young animals killed also implies that there must have been a good supply of milk available for human consumption, either fresh or in the form of butter or cheese. In the winter months

Ancient breeds of cattle at the Cotswold Farm Park in Gloucestershire

A breed of pig that closely resembles the Neolithic type

the cattle were probably bled, the blood being mixed with flour and herbs to make black puddings.

Pigs probably had less attention in Neolithic times and were allowed to forage at will through the forests until needed to supplement the food supply. Not only did they supply pork but also lard which was used in many dishes. Pigs may have sometimes been used, when confined in pens, to break up fallow land and manure it. If left long enough in a confined space they would even get rid of perennial weeds.

Sheep and goats were more important on higher ground, and they appear to have become more numerous during the later phases of British prehistory. Sheep were valued for mutton and wool while goats were probably kept for their milk as well as their meat.

Butter and cheese were milk products which could be kept for some time. Butter was probably made in much the same way as it was in the Orkneys until recent times. The milk was left to stand in the churn for two or three days until it thickened naturally. When the butter was slow in coming some red-hot 'Kirnin' stones were thrown in to help the separation process. When the butter had gathered at the top, it was lifted out into an earthenware dish and washed several times in cold water to remove any remaining milk, which would turn it sour quickly. It then had a knife passed through it several times to remove any animal hairs that would stick on the knife edge. In many parts of Britain it was the custom to bury the butter in wooden vessels or baskets, or occasionally in cloth, bark or leather containers, in peat bogs.

Soay sheep, probably the most primitive breed in the world having remained virtually unchanged since prehistoric times

Many discoveries of this 'bog butter' have been made, ranging in quantity from a few pounds to as much as a hundredweight. The most rational explanation for this is that the surplus summer butter was stored in the cool bog for use in the winter. One Irish writer records that unsalted butter flavoured with wild garlic used to be put in a boghole and left to ripen.

Cheese was made by heating thick cream and adding rennet, which was obtained from the stomachs of calves. Occasionally plants were used as a substitute for rennet: the leaves of butterwort (*Pinguicula vulgaris*), lady's bedstraw (*Galium verum*), and nettle juice have all been used for this purpose, the last two being used in making Double Gloucester cheese.

Simple cottage cheese can be made by standing the milk till it separates into curds and whey, straining the curds through a muslin bag overnight, and then emptying them into a bowl and adding chopped herbs and salt for flavour. My Cumbrian great-grandmother used to bury it in the garden for a week or so to improve the flavour. It should then be eaten fairly quickly as it does not keep well.

Together with their domestic animals, the Neolithic farmers brought bags of seed corn and introduced a range of crop plants.

They were the first people to cultivate the land and reap their harvests in autumn, storing it in pits to serve as the food supply through until the next harvest. Their chief crop was the hulled wheat called emmer, but they also grew a little einkorn wheat and brought two forms of the hulled six-row barley. Thus wheat and barley, which had first been domesticated in the Near East some thousands of years earlier, were introduced to the British Isles, and they still form our major cereals (although we now cultivate different species of wheat with better baking qualities). Oats and rye were not introduced, as far as we know, before the Iron Age, but spelt wheat may have been introduced before the end of the Bronze Age. The free-threshing forms of bread wheat were also known from this time onwards. The coarsely ground husked grains could have been baked into small unleavened loaves on the hearthstone beside the fire, or they could have been made into porridge or gruel, or added to stews or soups cooked in pots which the first farmers also introduced.

The weeds that grew in the cornfields were probably harvested with the grain and had a food value often comparable to that of the cereals. Moreover, they were often incorporated into the cereal-based pottage and added flavour to it. A richer, more interesting soup resulted from the addition of fat or oil to the pot. Animal fat, or the oil-bearing seeds of flax, would have been used. When the stomach contents of the Iron Age Tollund and Grauballe man were examined in Denmark, it was found that they had eaten a last meal which consisted of a cereal-based pottage mixed with linseed and a large number of weed seeds from a wide range of species. The stomach contents of Lindow man (see page 62) discovered in Cheshire provide direct evidence of the Iron Age diet in Britain.

Barley was also used for making malt and brewing beer. This process may well have been discovered by the end of the Neolithic period, and the appearance of elegant beakers indicate the popularity of this beverage. The process of making malt for the Orkney islands has been well described. Bere grain (hulled six-row barley) was set aside for malt. It was put in a large tub, covered with water and left to steep for 48 hours, then the water was drained off. The damp grain was spread out on the barn

Iron Age tankard made of bronze and wood from Trawsfynydd, Gwynned, North Wales

# LINDOW MAN

The discovery of the incredibly well-preserved body of a young Iron Age man in a peat bog at Lindow Moss in Cheshire has provided us with detailed knowledge of the diet at this period. Affectionately known as Pete Marsh, he was found in 1984 by some workmen who were digging out the peat for potting compost. Scientists who examined the

body revealed that he had eaten an unleavened 'bannock' made of wheat and barley and had drunk something containing a variety of plants including mistletoe.

It has been claimed that he was sacrificed in a horrific ritual – first he was knocked unconscious, then strangled with a knotted garotte and finally his throat was cut. The presence of mistletoe in his body, and the fact that he seems to have been a wealthy individual

whose well-manicured hands revealed that he had done no manual work, have led to the theory that he was a Druid prince who gave himself up willingly for sacrifice.

*Opposite:* A hologram provides a vivid image of the mummified body of Lindow Man

*Above:* Scientists have been able to build up a reconstruction of what Lindow Man would have looked like

floor for two or three days until germination took place. The grain was then collected in a heap, and two or three people began rubbing off the shoots with their feet by shuffling slowly round the heap, twisting their toes and heels alternately, working to the centre of the heap. The malt was again heaped up and covered with straw and a mat to induce heat and further fermentation – the grain showed renewed signs of life and emitted a strong liquorous smell. It was rubbed down again before being dried in the kiln. All that remained was the grinding of the malt on a quern. This was done in small quantities for immediate use while the rest was stored away in a dry place until required. The ground malt was put in a barrel and scalded with boiling water. After infusing for two hours the liquid was drawn off. For special occasions the ale was made more intoxicating by adding an oat sheaf to the must (some people preferred to add heather for this purpose). The liquor (wort) was boiled for about half an hour before being strained again, then cooled and set aside for some days to ferment with added yeast. When fermentation ceased the ale was drawn off and stored in barrels or bottles in a cool place.

The pulse crops – peas, beans and small broad beans – first appeared in Britain in the Bronze Age and, although they were useful

as a different type of seed crop which could be stored for use out of season and provide both starch and protein, they were never to become as popular crops as the cereals. They had two main uses as foodstuffs: when dried they could be ground up and added to cereal flour for bread-making in time of dearth and, more importantly, they could be used in soups and stews for when simmered in broth they burst open to absorb the broth and fat and become a palatable purée. Young peas could also be eaten fresh.

The surviving evidence sheds little light on the plant species which were collected and cooked as green vegetables. From finds of seeds we may however conclude that fat hen (*Chenopodium album*) was widely used as a green vegetable, probably cooked like spinach. Nettles, too, are well represented and may well have been gathered as young leaves and made into soups or eaten boiled. Other plants which have palatable leaves and may be cooked in these ways include

Cleavers, a plant with palatable leaves

common orache (*Atriplex patula*), easter ledge (*Polygonum bistorta*), white dead nettle (*Lamium album*), cleavers (*Galium aparine*), charlock (*Sinapis arvensis*) and wild cabbage (*Brassica oleracea*).

Edible roots may also have played a part as a source of food since early post-glacial times and were probably used in winter. The following species have been eaten in the more recent past: dandelion, wild parsnip, wild carrot, yellow goatsbeard, sow thistle and silverweed. A note of caution should be added – the roots are often rather small and those from old plants may be bitter or tough. The tuberous roots of the pignut (*Conopodium denudatum*) and the truffle (*Tuber aestivum*) have been regarded as delicacies. The roots of the couch grass (*Agropyron repens*) were used as famine food.

*Left:* Pignut and *right:* couch grass

In the early part of the year a number of young plants yield edible leaves suitable for use in salads. These include hairy bittercress, yellow rocket, ivy-leaved toadflax, lamb's lettuce, sorrel, wood sorrel, dandelion, red clover, wild basin, sow thistle, salad burnet (beware of its strong flavour) and wild marjoram. Remember that there was no oil or vinegar for the salad dressing.

Many wild plants have been used as herbs to add flavour to various dishes. We have definite evidence that the seeds of mustard, coriander and poppies were used as flavourings in prehistoric Britain. It is very likely that some of the following wild plants were also used. Onion flavour may be obtained from the new leaves and shoots of Jack-by-the-hedge (*Alliera petiola*) and the leaves and bulbs of wild garlic or ransoms (*Allium ursinum*). A peppery flavour can be obtained from all parts of wall pepper (*Sedum acre*) and also from lady's smock (*Cardamine pratensis*). Sorrel leaves (*Rumex acetosa*) have a vinegary flavour. The leaves of salad burnet (*Poterium sanguisorba*) taste rather like cucumber, and those of sweet cecily (*Myrrhis oderata*) have an aniseed

*Opposite:* Bunches of dried herbs hanging in a reconstructed roundhouse

Herb bennet

flavour. Corn mint (*Mentha arvensis*) tastes of mint while water mint tastes of peppermint. The roots of herb bennet (*Geum urbanum*) have a strong clove flavour, and all parts of tansy (*Chrysanthemum vulgare*) have a strong flavour of ginger. Juniper berries form a good savoury spice.

Pleasant drinks or tisanes can be made by pouring boiling water over the dried flowers of lime, elder, chamomile or woodruff, the fresh flowers of gorse, and mint leaves.

We have few remains of the mushrooms or fungi from our prehistoric past, but an interesting exception is the find of a number of mature puffballs in the midden of the Neolithic village of Skara Brae. These may have been discarded because they were overripe to use as food. Mushrooms are a useful source of food since they contain more protein than vegetables and a significant amount of vitamin D. They can easily be dried and stored for use out of season.

Before picking mushrooms to eat it is essential to become familiar with their identification: there are about 3,000 species of fungi growing in the British Isles and only 20 of them are poisonous, of which four are fatally so. The following species are edible and fairly easy to identify (please refer to a good manual if you are not absolutely sure) and they can be made into soups, added to stews or served in omelettes: morels, chanterelles, shaggy ink caps, saffron milk caps, shaggy parasols, ceps, blewits, field mushrooms, puffballs, beefsteak and oyster fungus.

All the fruits and nuts found on prehistoric sites in Britain belong to wild species. Many Mesolithic camp sites have yielded large numbers of hazelnuts, suggesting that they were collected for winter use. The native woodland was rich in fruit- and nut-bearing trees whose produce was eaten fresh in due season: acorns, beechmast, hazelnuts, sloes, rosehips, haws, rowan berries, crab apples, wild pears, elderberries, strawberries, blackberries and cranberries have all been found on prehistoric sites in Europe. In England, a beaker

# BOXGROVE MAN

An exciting discovery near the small West Sussex village of Boxgrove completely changed the interpretation of the Palaeolithic period in Britain. The site had been studied since 1985 but, in 1993, the first hominid fossil came to light. Dating to around 800,000 years ago these are the oldest hominid remains ever to be found in Britain and provided new evidence about how these earliest inhabitants looked and lived. Important information about food gathering and preparation was revealed by analysis of the large number of bones uncovered at the site. They indicated that animals such as horse and rhino were being eaten, and that these may well have been hunted

and killed with spears rather than scavenged. The fossil bones of a large horse skeleton showed that it had been carefully jointed and gutted using hand-axes as butchery tools. The meat would have been taken away for consumption – perhaps to the wooded areas near by, which were rich in berries, nuts and fungi to accompany the meal.

A reconstruction painting of Boxgrove by Peter Dunn

burial in the clay of the submerged coastline of Walton-on-the-Naze, Essex, was found to have a large quantity of fruit seeds in the stomach region: these were chiefly the seeds of blackberries, mixed with rosehips and the seeds of *Atriplex*. We know from the impressions of apple pips in their pottery that the first farmers ate crab apples. At Glastonbury the villagers had clearly been eating sloes – one mound produced nearly a barrow-load of sloe stones. All these fruits can be used to make a storable jelly. In most cases it is necessary to add an equal amount of crab apple to the fruit in order to get enough pectin to make the jelly set. It is made by first bringing the fruit to the boil and simmering until mushy, it is then strained through muslin to separate the juice from the fibres and seeds. Measure the volume of liquid obtained and then add an equal amount of honey to it. Bring to the boil, stirring well, and boil rapidly until the setting-point is reached (104°C/220°F on a jam thermometer). Pour into sterilised jars and cover with waxed paper. When cool, cover tightly and store in a cool place.

Crab apples may have been made into verjuice and cider in prehistoric times. Verjuice would have formed a useful substitute for vinegar which was not known before the advent of the Romans.

It is made by gathering the crab apples into a heap to sweat, discarding the stalks and any showing signs of decay. The apples are then mashed, using a cider press if possible to extract the juice. The liquid is then strained and stored for a month before it is ready for use. Crab apples were probably also halved and dried for use in the winter.

Honey was the only form of sweetening used in prehistoric Britain. We know from rock paintings that wild bees' nests were raided for honey in the late Palaeolithic period, and it seems likely that bees were actually being kept by the middle Bronze Age, for great quantities of wax were required for the casting of complex tools and weapons by the lost wax method. Wax would be useful to seal up jars of jelly, verjuice, ale and mead for storage. Honey and salt were traditionally used together to season roast meat and fish in Ireland.

Mead was almost certainly produced in prehistoric times. Honey, if left for a time, will ferment of itself, and honey and water left together in a container would have produced an alcoholic drink which could be flavoured with wild fruits and herbs. Traces of mead flavoured with cranberries and bog myrtle have been found in a birch bark container in a Bronze Age burial in Denmark. At Methilhill, near Kirkcaldy in Scotland, the pollen of small-leaved lime and meadowsweet was identified inside a beaker in a grave. It appears that the beaker originally held mead made from lime honey and flavoured with meadowsweet flowers. Interestingly, the small-leaved lime does not grow any nearer than the English Lake District, and so either the honey or mead had been transported quite a distance.

Pots with perforated bases have been noted at several Iron Age sites and it has been suggested that they were honey strainers for separating the comb wax from the honey; examples come from Glastonbury and All Cannings Cross.

A beaker and two beaker mugs displaying decorations that would have been made with a finely toothed comb

# COOKING TECHNIQUES
# AND UTENSILS

The use of preheated stones for cooking goes back at least to Mesolithic times and deposits of fire-cracked pebbles in small pits have been discovered in Oronsay. In the Bronze Age and later there is a whole category of sites known as 'mounds of burnt stones' which have been found from the New Forest in Hampshire to the Orkneys, as well as in Wales and southern Ireland. They appear to have been cooking places concerned with roasting or boiling meat. Quite often they are found associated with a large watertight trough in which the meat was boiled. The technique probably involved wrapping the meat in straw, tying it securely with straw ropes and then lowering it into boiling water in the trough. The water would have been brought to the boil by successively dropping in red-hot stones which had been heated in a log fire beside the trough. Other hot stones would be added to keep the temperature up until the meat was cooked.

Experiments have also revealed how meat could have been roasted in a stone-lined pit which had been preheated by burning brushwood inside it. After the ash was drawn out, the meat would have been placed inside and surrounded by a rough dome of red-hot stones, preheated in the fire. The covering stones would have needed changing several times during cooking time. The labour-intensive nature of the cooking must have given all concerned a good appetite.

The boiling of beef in a hide using pot boilers continued in some remote Scottish islands until the 18th century. One method used involved putting water into a block of wood which had been hollowed out with the help of a dirk and by burning. Then, using

fairly large stones heated red-hot and successively quenched in the vessel, the water was kept boiling until the food was completely cooked.

In the prehistoric huts on Dartmoor, each hut has a hearth sunk in the floor, and these are generally associated with heaps of fire-cracked pebbles, showing that

A prehistoric hearth in one of the roundhouses at Chysauster Ancient Village, Cornwall

pebbles heated in the hearth played an important part in cooking and in boiling water even round the domestic hearth. At Legis Tor a round-based pot was still in position in one of the stone-lined cooking holes, and had a fire-cracked flint inside it.

The usual way of cooking meat was by grilling or roasting it over the red-hot embers of the fire, using some sort of spit. This need not have been more elaborate than a straight green pole or stick, barbeque fashion, resulting in the meat having an appetizing charcoal flavour when ready to eat. By the Iron Age, elegant firedogs had been developed which may have also supported spits.

The need for large containers for making stews was met in the late Bronze Age by the introduction of huge bronze cauldrons and their related hooks, chains and tripods for suspension over the fire. The meat was fished out from these vessels with elaborate, long-handled flesh-hooks.

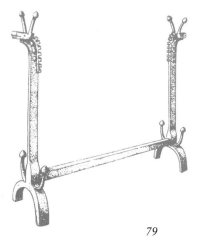

Iron Age firedog

79

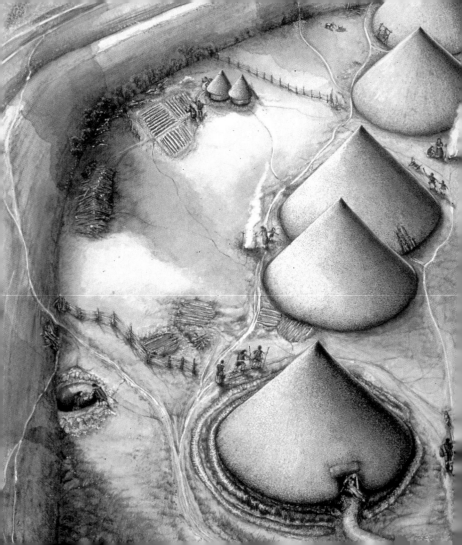

One of the most extraordinary features of the prehistoric houses which have been explored is their lack of ovens. It is not that our prehistoric ancestors did not know about ovens, since there are a number of examples from the Neolithic period in Orkney at the sites of Rinyo and the Links of Notland where there were small ovens beside the central hearth, but they were not found universally necessary. Even in the Iron Age, the villages of Glastonbury and Meare, where every house was furnished with a central hearth, have only two or three ovens in the whole village and these were probably associated with some occupation other than cooking food. The exception is at Maiden Castle in Dorset where three ovens were found in a single house. Thus, baking in ovens was not a commonly practised technique in prehistoric Britain.

*Opposite:* A painting by Miranda Schofield of what Maiden Castle might have looked like

*Right:* A reconstruction of a prehistoric oven

Baking appears to have been done on a flat stone or bakestone placed on or beside the central hearth. Sometimes bread may have been placed under an inverted pot which had hot embers piled over it. Flour made from emmer and einkorn wheat does not stretch very much in the dough, and so is better for making flat bread rather than leavened bread – although wild yeast may have been used to lighten the bread a little and add flavour.

The preparation of cereals for eating involved the use of pestles, mortars and querns. The houses at Skara Brae clearly show these two implements. The Neolithic querns were of the saddle type with a bun-shaped upper stone which was rubbed backwards and forwards over a flat stone base. Rotary querns were introduced only in the Iron Age. They consisted of two circular stones: the lower with a convex upper surface and the upper with a concave lower surface, and a central hole through which the grain was fed. At one side of the top stone a hole was drilled for the insertion of a wooden handle. The proximity of the two grindstones could be controlled by the insertion of leather washers

*Opposite:* A saddle-type quern

under the wooden crossbar. In more recent times in Orkney the washer was inserted when oatmeal or malt was being ground, but not for the grinding of the finer barley meal.

Grain could have been prepared in three ways. It could have been prepared like 'graddan' in the Hebrides up to the 18th century:

A rotary quern

a handful of ears of corn was held by the stalks over the flames, and the grains were beaten off at the moment when the husk was burnt but before the grain became charred. It was then winnowed and ground and baked within an hour of being harvested. Oats were 'burned in the sheaf' in a similar manner in Ireland in the past.

Another method was to make toasted grain, or 'burstin' as it is called in the Orkney islands. Barley grains were put in a pot beside the fire and the pot was tilted over on one side. To get the grains evenly fried and browned it was constantly stirred, and any which became burnt were discarded as they would give the burstin a dark colour and bitter taste. After being thoroughly toasted the grain was well sieved and then ground.

For making porridge or thickening soup the Orcadians used to use handfuls of threshed barley grains which were put in the 'knocking stane' or mortar with a little warm water, and were then lightly bruised with a mallet to break the husk. The husks were floated off by steeping in water and the grains were used just like pearl barley today. In the 19th century boiled cabbage and 'knocked corn' formed a substantial part of the diet of these islanders.

# SERVING PREHISTORIC FOOD

Apart from the flint-bladed knives there is little evidence of the eating equipment of our Mesolithic ancestors, although they may well have had containers made from leather or wood from which they ate their meals. The first farmers introduced the use of pottery for storing, cooking and eating their food. The earliest pottery forms were round-based undecorated bowls – gradually through time impressed decoration began to appear round the necks and shoulders of the bowls. The round bases would have been more practical on an uneven floor, and in houses with no table. By the late Neolithic period, two types of flat-based pots, decorated with grooves or impressions over most of their surfaces, had become fashionable: the so-called Peterborough and grooved ware. The finds of pottery ladles from Sussex suggest that spoons

*Right:* A bone finely toothed comb which could be used for decorating pottery

may also have been made of wood, bone or horn, and a wooden spurtle was found in a bowl associated with the Sweet Track in the Somerset Levels. A horn spoon was found in a beaker at Broomhead, Aberdeen.

The very finest prehistoric pottery made in Britain appeared in late Neolithic times in the form of beakers, which seem to have been drinking vessels and are usually found in graves. They are made from fine-grained clay and were decorated with horizontal bands of impression made with finely toothed combs. Some of these beakers have handles and look as if they are copies in clay of wooden tankards. We know that the beaker from Methilhill, Scotland, had contained mead. It is possible that they may also have been used for ale.

Drinking cups made from exotic materials are a feature of the early Bronze Age in Britain: the Rillaton cup

A grave beaker with impressed decoration made with a comb

was made of gold, the Hove cup was carved from a single piece of amber, and two cups carved from shale were found near Amesbury, Wiltshire. Whether these materials were used in order to reflect the importance of the people using them, or of the liquid to be drunk from them, is a matter of conjecture.

The Hove cup made from one piece of amber

The pottery of the early Bronze Age falls into two groups: the highly decorated flat-based, carinated bowls known as food vessels, and the larger urns with decorated rims and collars usually described as cinerary urns. Both are found associated with burials and so we cannot be sure that they have anything to do with food. Small 'incense' or pygmy vessels are frequently associated with the large urns and they often have holes for suspension and are decorated all over. Some are perforated while others have lids. They could have been used for salt since there is evidence for the exploitation of salt in East Anglia at least as far back as the early Bronze Age. It would have been extremely valuable as a condiment to add piquancy to the bland food usually cooked.

The late Bronze Age saw the introduction of beaten metal vessels – notably, from a culinary point of view, the cauldron and the bucket. At this time bronze knives were also being made, although flint continued to be used to make cutting tools into the Iron Age.

Some of the early Iron Age pottery was decorated with a bright red haematite slip to make it resemble the burnished bronze vessels which were still luxury items. Some of the decorated pottery of the middle and late Iron Age is also rather attractive, especially that manufactured in the villages of the Somerset Levels which is decorated with flowing lines and curvilinear patterns. The same style of decoration is also found on the wooden tub from Glastonbury. Here too were found both flint- and iron-bladed knives, and ladles and spoons made of wood. The curvilinear decoration is also to be found on the handles of bronze spoons which are characteristically found in pairs in Ireland and northern England, and also on the handles

*Right and opposite:* A pair of Iron Age spoons with cast iron decoration found at Penbryn, North Wales

of tankards, for example from Trawsfynydd, Gwynedd. The cast-iron firedogs such as those from Capel Garmon, Gwynedd; Welwyn, Hertfordshire and Lord's Bridge, Cambridgeshire, were also works of art with their animal head terminals, and serve to underline the importance of the hearth to the Iron Age chieftains. Cauldrons, their hooks, chains and tripods, also feature at this time and are often found in graves.

In the first century BC the potter's wheel was introduced and the pottery became much more stereotyped. Pedestalled bowls, platters, handled tankards and jars with countersunk handles became common pottery forms.

The rich burials of the Belgic chieftans show that already they had contact with the Roman world and were beginning to appreciate imported wine and olive oil. The grave goods found with the two burials uncovered at Welwyn at the beginning of the 20th century include Mediterranean amphorae which must have contained wine, together with bronze and silver vessels for serving and drinking wine, firedogs, spits and tripod cauldron hangers, pottery and wooden vessels – emphasising the importance of feasting and drinking.

Future excavations, especially of waterlogged habitation sites, will no doubt shed new light on foods, techniques of preparation, methods of cooking and serving of our prehistoric ancestors, but we have enough evidence to give us a glimpse into the way they utilised their available resources to provide an interesting and varied diet.

# BIBLIOGRAPHY

Ayrton, E., *The Cookery of England*, André Dutsch (London, 1974); Penguin Books (Harmondsworth, 1977).

Beeton, Mrs Isabella, *Mrs Beeton's Cookery and Household Management*, Ward Lock (London, 1960).

Cobbett, W., *Cottage Economy*, 1822, reprinted by Oxford University Press (Oxford, 1979).

David, E., *English Bread and Yeast Cookery*, Allen Lane and Penguin Books (Harmondsworth, 1977).

Drummond, J.C., and Wilbraham, A., *The Englishman's Food*, Jonathan Cape (London, 1939).

Grigson, G., *The Englishman's Flora*, Phoenix House (London, 1958; Paladin (St Albans, 1975).

Grigson, J., English Food, Macmillan (London, 1974); Penguin Books (Harmondsworth, 1977).

—, *Jane Grigson's Fruit Book*, Michael Joseph (London, 1982); Penguin Books (Harmondsworth, 1983).

Hill, J., *The Wild Foods of Britain*, A. and C. Black (Publishers) Ltd (London, 1939).

Mabey, R., *Food for Free*, Collins (London, 1972); Fontana (London, 1976).

Phillips, R., *Wild Food*, Pan Books (London, 1983).

Richardson, R., *Hedgerow Cookery*, Penguin Books (Harmondsworth, 1980).

Simmons, J., *A Shetland Cook Book*, Thuleprint Ltd (Sandwick, Shetland, 1978).

Stout, M.B., *The Shetland Cookery Book*, T. and J. Manson (Lerwick, 1968).

Wilson, C. A., *Food and Drink in Britain*, Constable (London, 1973); Penguin Books (Harmondsworth, 1976).

## ACKNOWLEDGEMENTS

The publishers would like to thank Christine Shaw for permission to use Butser Ancient Farm, near Petersfield, Hampshire, and to David Freeman of Gallica. We are grateful to James O Davies and Peter Williams for taking many of the photographs included in this book, and to Dr David Jones for his advice.

We would like to thank the following people and organisations listed below for permission to reproduce the photographs in this book. Every care has been taken to trace copyright holders, but any omission will, if notified, be corrected in any future edition.

All photographs are © English Heritage or © Crown copyright.NMR with the exception of the following: Front cover, p9, p18, p19 Bridgeman Art Library; p10 Musee d'Unterlinden, Colmar, France, Lauros, Giraudon/Bridgeman Art Library; p25 Maximilian Stock Ltd/Science Photo Library; p31, p55, p56, p57 Cotswold Farm Park, Guiting Power, Gloucestershire; p62, p63 British Museum/ Munoz-Yague/Science Photo Library; p78 Max Alexander; p89 Royal Pavilion, Libraries and Museums, Brighton & Hove; p91 Ashmolean Museum, University of Oxford, UK/Bridgeman Art Library; back cover Chris Hull.

# RECIPE INDEX

Other titles in this series:

Roman Cookery

Medieval Cookery

Tudor Cookery

Stuart Cookery

Georgian Cookery

Victorian Cookery

Ration Book Cookery

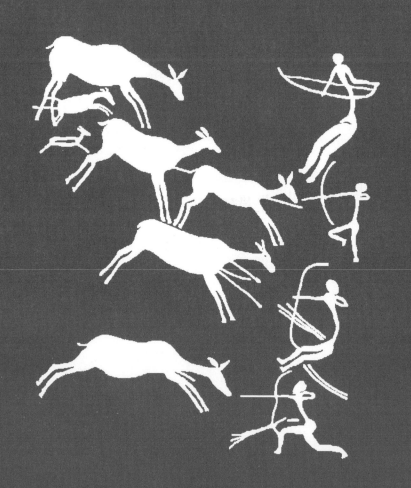